a SAVOR THE SOUTH™ *cookbook*

Buttermilk

a SAVOR THE SOUTH™ *cookbook*

Buttermilk

DEBBIE MOOSE

The University of North Carolina Press CHAPEL HILL

The paper in this book meets the guidelines for permanence and durability of
the Committee on Production Guidelines for Book Longevity of the Council on
Library Resources. The University of North Carolina Press has been a member
of the Green Press Initiative since 2003.

Library of Congress Cataloging-in-Publication Data
Moose, Debbie.
Buttermilk : a savor the South™ cookbook / Debbie Moose. — 1 [edition].
p. cm.
Includes index.
ISBN 978-0-8078-3578-4 (cloth : alk. paper)
1. Cooking (Sour cream and milk) 2. Buttermilk.
3. Cooking, American — Southern style. I. Title.
TX759.5.S68M66 2012   641.6′7148 — dc23
2012002037

16 15 14 13 12   5 4 3 2 1

To Rob

You're still the sweet-yet-tart center

of my life

Contents

Sweet Endings   53

PIES, CAKES, ICE CREAMS, AND OTHER DELIGHTS

Good Things Anytime   71
DIPS, DRESSINGS, AND DRINKS

a SAVOR THE SOUTH™ *cookbook*

Buttermilk

Introduction

Like a full moon on a warm southern night, buttermilk makes something special happen. The magical touch of buttermilk creates fluffy pancakes, sweet cakes, and cooling soups. It's the special ingredient for tart ice creams and curry chicken marinades. Buttermilk can become Italian or German cheese. It lends a refreshing flavor to Indian beverages. If you're one of those people who doesn't like the "fishy" flavor of fish, you need to keep buttermilk in your refrigerator because it mellows the strong taste.

Sure, other things, like moonshine and sweet iced tea, may spring to mind more quickly than buttermilk when thinking about iconic southern liquids. But can a shot of Kentucky bourbon do as much in the kitchen as buttermilk? I don't think so.

Buttermilk is truly representative of the South—both the traditional South of country farms and the evolving region of creative chefs and international influences. And I believe that buttermilk is an essential ingredient for cooking of all kinds. Without it, there would be no cloud-soft biscuits in which to insert country ham. No silky buttermilk pies. And, heavens, no tender-crispy fried chicken.

In agrarian times, buttermilk was simply the liquid that remained after the butter had been churned out of fresh cream (using an old wooden butter churn and plenty of arm power). So, in a way, the name is a little confusing—I guess it should have been called "no-butter" milk, although a little bit of the butterfat remained behind. But there is much more to the process than just the churning, especially in modern dairy production.

However, the qualities that make buttermilk good for cooking haven't changed. The best buttermilk starts with the best milk, of course, and the South is lucky to be seeing a growth in small dairies that produce quality milk. Seek them out to find buttermilk that is rich and thick, with a pleasantly sour flavor reminiscent of yogurt. In fact, good-quality buttermilk — that nice and thick kind — can be substituted for yogurt in recipes. Be sure to adjust the recipe to handle the additional liquid so there is no change in the dish's texture. Yogurt can be a stand-in for buttermilk, too, with the addition of a little liquid.

Read on and I'll tell you about ways to create magic with buttermilk in your own kitchen. My recipes will allow you to bring buttermilk into your life all day long, from breakfast through dinner to sweets and snacks. You'll learn about the history of buttermilk in southern cooking and how today's food fans continue to explore the ingredient. You'll get tips on selecting and using buttermilk so that you get the best flavor in your dishes. Not all buttermilks are the same.

Why Buttermilk?

Many people have asked me why I wanted to write an entire cookbook about buttermilk. My first encounter with buttermilk was the same as that for many southerners — seeing my father crumble leftover cornbread into a tall glass, then fill it with buttermilk that was left in the refrigerator after making the cornbread. I tried a spoonful from his glass. It tasted really different, with the chunky texture and lip-puckering flavor of the buttermilk, especially for a kid. (Making that snack was also the closest my father ever came to cooking; he could barely heat up canned soup.) Cornbread was one of the few things my mother would take the time to make from scratch, and she always purchased buttermilk for it. So I grew up thinking that it was a rare but sometimes absolutely necessary thing.

As an adult, after the first time I made buttermilk pancakes for breakfast, there was no going back. Not only did that single ingredient lift average pancakes to a different plane in flavor, but it made them as fluffy and light as a dream. I wanted to know more about that sorcerer buttermilk.

Also, as fabulous as cornbread and pancakes are, I wanted to help people think beyond them, to answer the question that I've been asked so many times while writing this book: "What am I supposed to do with the rest of that carton of buttermilk in my refrigerator?" There is so much, people, so much you can do. I've even talked to some who use it instead of regular milk in their breakfast cereal.

What Is Buttermilk?

Let's start with how the magic happens. What is buttermilk, exactly? The traditional answer is that it's what's left after the butter is churned from cream, but the process is more complicated than that. I turned to Lynn G. Turner, emeritus professor of food sciences in the Department of Food, Bioprocessing and Nutrition Sciences at North Carolina State University in Raleigh, for the complete picture.

The old wooden butter churn uses gravity to separate the butter from cream, and the motion of churning makes the fat globules in the cream come together. As the butter forms, the pH of the liquid drops, meaning that it becomes more acidic. The texture and proteins change, and the butter becomes more gel-like as it forms. Churning removes as much liquid as possible from the butter, which typically is about 80 percent fat. After the butter is gone, what remains is the buttermilk, which is fairly acidic and still contains a small amount of fat.

In the days before refrigeration, buttermilk was left sitting out—frugal southerners would never throw it away. That's when the second part of making buttermilk would take place. Bacteria in the air and on the wooden churn paddle would change the lactose in the buttermilk to lactic acid, and natural fermentation would take place. "You hoped the good bacteria outnumbered anything that might cause food-borne illness problems," Turner explained.

In the hot weather of the South, fresh raw milk had a very short shelf life. Natural fermentation would extend the usable life of the buttermilk, and southerners came to relish the tart flavor.

Today, most of the buttermilk you find in supermarkets is not produced by churning. Dairies create it by adding commercial cultures to what older southerners call "sweet milk." Usually, dairies add two different cultures — there are several to choose from — to change the lactose to lactic acid. The cultures do what letting a pitcher sit on the kitchen counter used to do, but in a more controlled manner — they cause the fermentation that gives buttermilk its tart flavor and typical buttery aroma. "The quality of cultured buttermilk depends on the raw material, the length of fermentation, the temperature, the type of culture. It's like making wine or cheese," Turner said.

Before manufacturers add the cultures, they give the milk a heat treatment similar to the one used to make yogurt, according to *On Food and Cooking: The Science and Lore of the Kitchen* by Harold McGee (Scribner, 2004). At the proper time, the milk is cooled to stop the fermentation and gently agitated to break up the curds that form to create a smooth, thick liquid.

A variation on the typical process produces "Bulgarian buttermilk." Yogurt cultures are added to or replace the typical cream cultures to produce a more acidic buttermilk that resembles yogurt.

Before Buttermilk, There Was Milk

Some wines and cheeses are better than others, and it's the same with buttermilk. Some kinds are thick and rich additions to cooking, others thin impersonators. How can you tell the good ones? To talk about buttermilk quality, we have to look at the milk it comes from.

In the 1880s, centrifuges were used for the first time to separate cream from milk. Until then, you let the milk simply sit until the fat separated — hence the saying "Cream rises to the top." Bottled milk would have a thick plug of cream at the top, requiring it to be shaken up for each use.

Shortly after the use of centrifuges became widespread, scientists invented a test to determine the precise fat content of milks from different sources, according to Anne Mendelson, *Milk: The Surprising Story of Milk through the Ages* (Alfred A. Knopf,

2008). Combine these factors with the growth of homogenization, which keeps milk fat dispersed throughout the milk, and the result was the ability to develop different kinds of milk with precise levels of fat.

Today, industrial-scale milk production starts with removing all the fat from the milk. Then the fat is added back in amounts that meet industry standards for fat-free milk, 2-percent-fat milk, or whole milk. Some of that milk eventually becomes buttermilk. Some small dairy farmers say that this process, plus the heat involved in high-temperature pasteurization, damages the flavor of buttermilk.

"We make whole-milk buttermilk. That's the problem with buttermilk today, that there is no whole milk today," said Tom Trantham, owner of Happy Cow Creamery, a small organic dairy in Pelzer, South Carolina. "When you homogenize and take the cream out, then squirt some back in, you've already damaged the milk and it can't function like it's supposed to. We don't take anything out."

What industrial milk production means for buttermilk is that the carton you pick up in the supermarket dairy case could have any level of fat content, and the flavor and texture will vary widely. Read the label to check the amount of fat. For most cooking, especially baking, buttermilk with some fat — even better, full fat — will provide better results than fat-free versions.

You'll also find that drinking full-fat buttermilk from a small dairy, if you can find it, is an entirely different experience. It's almost like yogurt, with satisfying thickness and appealing tang. Look for buttermilk from small farms for better cooking as well.

Singing the Praises of Buttermilk

Thick glasses of buttermilk have sustained many southerners on days when there wasn't much else to eat, so it shouldn't be surprising that it has worked its way into song and literature.

The most famous musical offering involving buttermilk is "Ole Buttermilk Sky," written in 1946 by Hoagy Carmichael. The songwriter was born in Indiana, but southerners should be willing to claim him because he also wrote the beautiful "Georgia on My Mind."

"Buttermilk sky" is an old term for a sky that's covered in rows of small, lumpy puffs of clouds that look like the curds of thick, old-time buttermilk. In the tune, the singer is going to meet his love and plans to pop the question if he can get a little help from above — a plea for the buttermilk sky to work its magic. Both Willie Nelson and 1940s bandleader and Chapel Hill, North Carolina, native Kay Kyser have recorded the tune as well. Here's a piece of buttermilk trivia: Mike Douglas, who eventually became a talk-show host, sang on Kyser's recording of the tune.

While we're singing about buttermilk, let's dance to it, too. Most versions of the playground favorite "Skip to My Lou" include a lyric about a fly in the buttermilk. The tune was popular at frontier parties in the 1800s, and its roots are likely Scottish. Both in Scotland and the American frontier, buttermilk was a part of cooking, and it was just natural to sing about it.

Southern literature is awash in buttermilk. Characters in William Faulkner's novels wash down turnip greens with it, carry it in Thermoses for lunch, and wrap jugs of it in wet gunnysacks to keep it cold for traveling. (See *Go Down Moses*, *The Reivers*, and *As I Lay Dying*, to name just a few.) It shows up so much that you could forget that Faulkner's favorite beverage was bourbon.

You'll find characters sipping buttermilk in the fiction of Walker Percy, Truman Capote, and Eudora Welty, who writes about the "buttermilk man" hawking buttermilk and dewberries as he walks the streets of a small southern town.

Besides including buttermilk in fiction because it was typically found in rural southern homes, authors also may have used it in many works to suggest that a character represented the common man.

Poet Maya Angelou once said: "'Public' and 'poem' go together like buttermilk and champagne." But she changed her mind enough about the public consumption of poetry to write poems commemorating President Bill Clinton's inauguration and other events. And I know some bartenders who might take that comparison as a challenge.

Cooking with Buttermilk

As much as we love buttermilk in the South, we can't claim exclusive ownership of the ingredient. Fermented milks such as yogurt and buttermilk are widely used all over the world. In India, lassi is a smoothie-like beverage that contains buttermilk or yogurt combined with ice or water. Usually savory flavors are preferred over sweet ones, although mango lassi is popular.

Quark, a cheese made from buttermilk, is a staple in Scandinavian, German, and Eastern European cooking. It is similar in texture to a creamy ricotta cheese, and its name comes from the German word for "curd." Quark is sometimes flavored with herbs or garlic. Its mildly tart flavor — thanks to buttermilk — is great on a baked potato or paired with sweet roasted beets in a salad.

Russian and Polish cooking is full of cold beet and cucumber soups that are enriched with the tang of creamy buttermilk. In Morocco, meals often end with cooled, sweetened couscous mixed with cold buttermilk.

A variation on buttermilk, kefir, originated in the Caucasus Mountains between Europe and Asia. A complex fermentation process makes kefir effervescent, tart, and slightly alcoholic, according to McGee's *On Food and Cooking*.

In the South, older cookbooks that mention "sour milk" as an ingredient usually are talking about buttermilk. A century or more ago, it was something that southern families just had in the house and used because it was on hand, perhaps without specific recipes at all.

Buttermilk took on a new role around 1800 with the advent of chemical leavening as a quicker alternative to yeast for baking, according to Mendelson's *Milk*. These ancestors of baking soda were alkaline leaveners, so they required the addition of an acid ingredient to produce the carbon dioxide that makes breads and cakes rise. And there was acidic buttermilk, just waiting to do the job. Plus, it added its unique flavor to the dish. The usefulness of buttermilk in baking with the new leaveners led to the appearance of cultured buttermilk, which has been sold in grocery stores since the 1920s.

The quality of the buttermilk you can buy today varies, and you will notice the difference. One of the few dairies in the United States that still combines churning with culturing is Cruze Dairy Farm near Knoxville, Tennessee. Cruze buttermilk, which is craved by southern chefs, is almost as thick as yogurt and has a rich flavor. Compare it to the thin gruel of some mass-produced buttermilk, and you'll see the ingredient's possibilities.

Many small southern dairies, like Cruze, are restoring buttermilk's good name. Some are as secretive as the CIA about how they produce their buttermilk. "You'd be giving away my trade secrets," said Tom Trantham of Happy Cow Creamery when I asked how he makes it. "We do have a paddle in our pasteurizer. We use the finest culture money can buy, salt, and our milk. That's it." He starts with whole milk from his grass-fed cows (no fat-free buttermilk here), which is pasteurized at the lowest safe temperatures to preserve the flavor.

He pays homage to buttermilk at the creamery's store by offering a twist on the classic southern treat of cornbread and buttermilk: cheddar Goldfish crackers and buttermilk, combined in a Mason jar with a stem like a wine glass and stirred with a silver spoon.

The return of quality buttermilk is inspiring chefs and food fans all over the South to use it in new ways. Olive & Sinclair, an artisan chocolate company in Nashville, Tennessee, has created a buttermilk–white chocolate bar. "Just being southern, I love the tang that buttermilk has, and one thing that white chocolate is missing is there's no bite to balance it out. I thought that would be awesome. That would be the best thing since white chocolate was invented. We started making small batches and it really worked," said owner Scott Witherow.

Even chefs who don't cook with southern accents have seized the mystical power of buttermilk. Andrea Reusing, who cooks with a definitely Asian touch at her restaurant Lantern in Chapel Hill, uses the ingredient quite a bit. "We do a couple of different cold soups, we dredge catfish in it and occasionally chicken, we do a ton of pastries and chickpea dumplings for an Indian stew, using chickpea flour and different spices," she said.

Tips for Using Buttermilk

Now it's time for you to try this at home.

* Look for the best thick and tangy buttermilk you can find. Fat content varies, so read the label. A higher fat content will make a difference especially in the richness of ice creams. Try to find buttermilk that does not have added gums or stabilizers and has active cultures, especially if you want to use it to make homemade cheeses; those that do will say "active cultures" or "live cultures" on the label. Whatever kind of buttermilk you purchase, shake it well before using because it can separate.

* Because buttermilk is cultured and fermented, it curdles easily when heated, more easily than milk or cream. If you must heat it for a dish, place it on low heat just until it feels warm when you dip in a finger. Avoid stirring it directly into very hot dishes, such as hot soups. Mixing the buttermilk with a little flour before heating may help.

* Because buttermilk is cultured, like yogurt, it will keep longer in the refrigerator than regular milk. It does not freeze well, however.

* Powdered or dried buttermilk, available in canisters, is useful in baking when you want buttermilk's flavor but don't want to add liquid. Refrigerate open canisters to keep the contents fresh.

* To make a substitute for buttermilk, add 1 tablespoon of lemon juice or white vinegar to 1 cup of milk, then let it stand for five minutes, until the milk curdles from the acid of the vinegar. You will get an approximation of buttermilk by doing this, but it's a pale shadow of the real thing.

* You can substitute buttermilk and its wonderful tart flavor for milk or cream in many recipes. (And a little added to piecrust makes it tender.) Just remember that buttermilk has a higher acid level than milk or cream, and depending on the kind of buttermilk you buy, it may have different fat content. In baking, if the recipe includes baking powder or

baking soda, either will react with buttermilk's acid to make the baked good rise. If you're using a large amount of buttermilk, you could increase the baking soda by a small amount if you're unsure — ¼ teaspoon or less.

* Buttermilk may be used in recipes instead of yogurt, but because buttermilk is thinner, be aware that it may change the texture of the resulting dish. If making the switch the other way, from buttermilk to yogurt, you may need to add a little water to thin the yogurt.

* Give whipped cream a different flavor by substituting buttermilk for part of the heavy cream. Start with about one-quarter to one-third of the total amount of cream. Because buttermilk has a lower fat content, it would be difficult to make whipped cream from buttermilk alone.

* According to the Academy of Nutrition and Dietetics, consuming small amounts of buttermilk that contains live and active cultures (check the label because not all buttermilks contain them) can help people with lactose intolerance digest lactose.

* It is possible to make your own butter at home, which means you'd make buttermilk as well. Andrea Reusing's staff at Lantern gave her a hand-powered butter churn as a lark. She used it to make butter for a special event — there's no way she could make all the butter for the restaurant — and did get a bit of buttermilk. She cultured it like yogurt and used it to make pancakes for her kids. It would take a lot of churning, or time in the food processor, to get an appreciable amount of buttermilk, though. If you want to try it, use cream that hasn't been ultra-high-temperature pasteurized (UHT on labels) if you can find it, advised North Carolina State University's Lynn Turner. Turner said it is possible to make buttermilk at home using a process similar to the way you make homemade yogurt. "Get milk of any kind, then add buttermilk that has active cultures and it will ferment the milk," he said. "There's a lot on the web about that."

Here are some things that I bet you never knew about buttermilk.

* Mama always said that buttermilk would take away freckles. Well, that wasn't true, but the astringent quality of buttermilk coupled with moisture from the fat it contains make it a mild, refreshing cleanser. Try it, since you'll have some around from cooking anyway. Bring 1 cup of water to a boil, then remove the pan from the heat and add 1 tablespoon of dried lavender buds. Let it sit for 30 minutes, then strain out all the lavender. Stir in 1 teaspoon of honey and 1 tablespoon of buttermilk until the mixture is combined. Apply the cleanser to your face with a cotton ball, then rinse afterward, just as you would with any facial cleanser. Store the cleanser in the refrigerator (I use a glass jar with a screw top), and shake or stir it before using to recombine it. The lavender is optional, but it adds a soothing aroma.
* Legend says that Cleopatra kept her skin beautiful by soaking in milk-and-honey baths. Considering the heat of Alexandria, her rubber duckie was probably floating in buttermilk. I can't say that buttermilk baths will turn you into the queen of Egypt, but you could try tossing some powdered buttermilk into your bath for a moisturizing, calming soak. Add a few drops of vanilla extract for a pleasant scent.
* If you wanted to paint your barn in the colonial era, you couldn't run down to the hardware store and grab a gallon of red. Farmers used natural pigments found on the farm mixed with, you guessed it, buttermilk. Modern manufacturers use powdered milk to reproduce the flat, matte finish of the surprisingly durable antique milk paint.
* Another installment in "Unusual Things Buttermilk Can Do" comes from a friend of mine. Her elementary school teacher had the class use colored chalk dipped in buttermilk as paint. It works as well on paper as tempera paints, without the danger of tipping over pots of paint and dirty water or spattering tables with brushes.

In the Morning

BREAKFAST RECIPES TO START THE DAY

Buttermilk offers many great ways to start
the day. Try pancakes, scones, cinnamon rolls, or
crispy doughnuts, and you'll be rarin' to go.

Craig's Sweet Potato Pancakes with Orange Butter

There are no tomatoes in these pancakes, despite the fact that Craig LeHoullier of Raleigh, North Carolina, is known as Tomato-man for his expertise with heirloom tomatoes. When he's not growing tomatoes or planning tomato-related events, he's cooking good things like this.

MAKES 14–16 PANCAKES

4 tablespoons unsalted butter, at room temperature

2 teaspoons grated orange zest

2 cups all-purpose flour (see Note below)

$\frac{1}{2}$ teaspoon salt

$1\frac{1}{2}$ teaspoons baking soda

1 teaspoon baking powder

$\frac{1}{4}$ cup sugar

1 teaspoon nutmeg

1 tablespoon cinnamon

$\frac{1}{4}$ teaspoon cloves

$\frac{1}{4}$ teaspoon ground ginger

$\frac{1}{2}$ cup chopped pecans, toasted (optional)

1 cup mashed cooked sweet potato

2 tablespoons melted unsalted butter

2 large eggs, separated

2 cups buttermilk

Maple syrup, for serving

To prepare the Orange Butter, using a fork or a food processor, combine the room-temperature butter and orange zest. Refrigerate until needed. This may be made a day ahead.

In a large bowl, combine the flour, salt, baking soda, baking powder, sugar, nutmeg, cinnamon, cloves, ginger, and pecans, if using.

In a medium bowl, whisk together the sweet potato, melted butter, egg yolks, and buttermilk. In a separate bowl, beat the egg whites until they form soft peaks.

Pour the buttermilk mixture into the dry ingredients. Mix quickly with a large spoon. Do not overmix; a few lumps are OK. Use a spatula to gently fold the beaten whites into the batter until they are incorporated.

Use a ¼-cup measure to pour the batter into a nonstick pan on medium heat. The batter will be thick; use a spoon or the back of the measuring cup to spread it out a little and don't set the heat too high. Cook until lightly browned on both sides.

Serve with Orange Butter and maple syrup.

NOTE ❋ You can substitute 1 cup whole wheat flour for 1 cup of the all-purpose flour, if you like. Also, I think a drop or two of Grand Marnier wouldn't hurt that Orange Butter one bit.

Bananaville Bread

This is my famous-since-2010 recipe that was inspired by a cold afternoon and a bowl of overripe bananas. It's a trip to the islands in a quick bread.

MAKES 1 LOAF

½ cup chopped walnuts or pecans
¾ cup flaked coconut
½ cup unsalted butter, at room temperature
   (see Note below)
⅔ cup sugar
2 large eggs
3 tablespoons dark rum
½ teaspoon vanilla
¼ cup buttermilk
2 cups all-purpose flour
1 teaspoon baking powder
½ teaspoon baking soda
½ teaspoon salt
1 cup mashed ripe banana
¼ cup crushed pineapple, well drained

Preheat the oven to 350°. Spread the nuts and coconut in a large pan and toast in the oven for a few minutes, stirring occasionally. Spray a 9 × 5-inch loaf pan with nonstick cooking spray.

Using a stand mixer on medium speed, cream the butter and sugar. Beat in the eggs, rum, vanilla, and buttermilk.

In another bowl, combine the flour, baking powder, baking soda, and salt. Mix into the creamed butter and sugar on medium speed. When combined, add the banana, toasted nuts and coconut, and pineapple.

Pour the batter into the prepared pan, then bake for 50–60 minutes or until a toothpick inserted into the center comes out clean. Cool in the pan on a wire rack for about 15 minutes, then turn the bread out onto the rack and cool completely before storing or freezing.

NOTE ❋ You can increase the tropical flavor by substituting ½ cup naturally refined, organic, nonhydrogenated coconut oil for the butter.

Irish Buttermilk Bread

Irish roots run deep in North Carolina and throughout the South. Traditional Irish soda bread is simpler and drier than my version, which is sweet and rich. Many recipes include caraway seeds, but you can easily omit them if you don't like the flavor.

MAKES 1 LOAF

2 cups all-purpose flour
½ cup sugar
3 teaspoons baking powder
½ teaspoon baking soda
½ teaspoon salt
6 tablespoons cold unsalted butter
½ cup raisins
1 tablespoon caraway seeds
1¼ cups buttermilk

Preheat the oven to 350°. Spray a 9 × 5-inch loaf pan with non-stick cooking spray. In a large bowl, stir together the flour, sugar, baking powder, baking soda, and salt. Cut the butter into the dry ingredients with a pastry blender until no large chunks remain. Stir in the raisins and caraway seeds. Mix in the buttermilk. The batter will be thick, like a biscuit dough.

Pour the batter into the prepared pan. Bake for 45 minutes or until a toothpick inserted into the center comes out clean. Cool in the pan on a wire rack for about 15 minutes. Remove the bread from the pan and serve warm, or turn the bread out onto the rack and cool completely before storing or freezing.

Cinnamon Spice Muffins

Every southern woman has go-to recipes that she can whip up when she needs to carry something to a potluck or receives an impromptu invitation to brunch. This is one of mine. If you do manage to think ahead, the muffins freeze well; just cool them completely and seal them in airtight bags. The magic of buttermilk keeps them moist.

MAKES ABOUT 12 MUFFINS

½ cup unsalted butter, at room temperature
¾ cup sugar
1 large egg
2 cups all-purpose flour
½ teaspoon baking soda
½ teaspoon baking powder
2 teaspoons cinnamon
½ teaspoon mace or nutmeg
1 cup buttermilk

Preheat the oven to 350°. Spray a 12-muffin tin with nonstick cooking spray. In the bowl of a stand mixer, cream the butter and sugar. Add the egg and mix well. In a separate bowl, sift together the flour, baking soda, baking powder, cinnamon, and mace or nutmeg. With the mixer on low, alternate adding the flour mixture and the buttermilk to the egg mixture, beginning and ending with flour.

Distribute the batter evenly in the muffin pan. Bake for 30–45 minutes or until a toothpick inserted into the center of a muffin comes out clean. Cool for 5 minutes or so on a wire rack before removing the muffins from the pan.

BBB Scones

You know how it is. You're having a fiddle lesson, and the next thing you know, you and your teacher are talking about food. The result from one such lesson was these scones. The three Bs are buttermilk, buckwheat flour, and bacon, because bacon makes everything better. Use a good smoky bacon for the best flavor.

MAKES 8 SCONES

½ cup buckwheat flour

1½ cups all-purpose flour

½ cup firmly packed brown sugar

1½ teaspoons baking powder

½ teaspoon baking soda

¼ teaspoon salt

½ teaspoon cinnamon

6 tablespoons cold unsalted butter

½ cup cooked, well-drained, crumbled smoky bacon
(about 6 slices)

1 large egg

1 cup buttermilk

½ teaspoon vanilla

Preheat the oven to 400°. Lightly spray a cookie sheet with nonstick cooking spray. In a large bowl, stir together the flours, sugar, baking powder, baking soda, salt, and cinnamon. You may want to use a fork or pastry blender to break up the sugar. Cut the cold butter into cubes and scatter them over the dry ingredients. Use a pastry blender to cut the butter into the dry ingredients until the mixture resembles coarse cornmeal. Stir in the bacon.

In a separate bowl, whisk together the egg, buttermilk, and vanilla. Stir into the dry ingredients until the dough comes together. Add a bit more buttermilk if needed to make a moist but not soggy dough.

Turn the dough out onto the cookie sheet and gently pat it out, with lightly floured fingers, into a circle about ½-inch thick. Score the dough into 8 wedges with a serrated knife.

Bake for 15 minutes or until golden brown. Cool on a wire rack before serving.

Chocolate Chip Buttermilk Scones

When I saw the Stone of Scone at Westminster Abbey in London, I didn't think it looked anything like the breakfast goodie I enjoy. And I know mine tastes better. This recipe also provides an excuse to have chocolate for breakfast. Like you need one.

MAKES 8 SCONES

2 cups all-purpose flour
$\frac{1}{2}$ cup sugar
$1\frac{1}{2}$ teaspoons baking powder
$\frac{1}{2}$ teaspoon baking soda
$\frac{1}{4}$ teaspoon salt
6 tablespoons cold unsalted butter
$\frac{1}{2}$ cup mini chocolate chips
$\frac{1}{2}$ cup buttermilk
1 large egg
1 teaspoon vanilla

Preheat the oven to 400°. Spray a cookie sheet with nonstick cooking spray. Stir together the flour, sugar, baking powder, baking soda, and salt in a large bowl. Cut the cold butter into small cubes and scatter them over the dry ingredients. Use a pastry blender to cut the butter into the dry ingredients until the result looks like coarse cornmeal. Don't overblend. Add the mini chocolate chips and, using two large spoons, gently and quickly toss them with the other ingredients.

In another bowl, whisk together the buttermilk, egg, and vanilla. Stir into the dry ingredients. The mixture will be sticky. Lightly flour your hands, then turn the dough out onto the cookie sheet and gently pat it out into a circle about 8 inches in diameter. Score the dough into 8 wedges with a serrated knife.

Bake for about 20 minutes or until the top is lightly browned and a toothpick inserted into the scones comes out clean. Cool on a wire rack before serving.

Tupelo Honey Cafe's Ginormous Biscuits

No false advertising here — these airy biscuits are huge. They have also drawn big numbers of fans to this Asheville, North Carolina, restaurant, where biscuits aren't just for breakfast. The recipe is printed with permission from Tupelo Honey Cafe: Spirited Recipes from Asheville's New South Kitchen *by Elizabeth Sims with Chef Brian Sonoskus (Kansas City: Andrews McMeel Publishing, 2011).*

MAKES 6 BISCUITS

2 cups bread flour
1 tablespoon baking powder
$\frac{1}{4}$ teaspoon baking soda
2 tablespoons sour cream
$1\frac{1}{2}$ teaspoons salt
$\frac{3}{4}$ cup frozen unsalted butter
About $\frac{1}{2}$ cup buttermilk
1 tablespoon melted unsalted butter

Preheat the oven to 450°. Combine the flour, baking powder, baking soda, sour cream, and salt in a large bowl. With a cheese grater, grate the frozen butter using the largest holes; quickly cut the butter into the flour mixture with a pastry cutter or fork until the mixture resembles coarse cornmeal. Add the buttermilk to the flour mixture and stir just until combined. If the dough does not come together, add a bit more buttermilk. Do not overmix.

On a floured surface, turn out the dough and roll out to a 1-inch thickness. Using a 3-inch biscuit cutter, cut the biscuits and place them on a rimmed sheet pan. Cook on the top rack of the oven for about 20 minutes, or until light brown, and remove from the oven. Brush the melted butter on top of each biscuit and return to the oven for about 5 minutes longer, or until the biscuits are golden brown.

Cinnamon-Raisin Rolls

Who can resist the aroma of cinnamon rolls at the mall? I can, because mine are so much tastier. Buttermilk brings the goodness and even allows you to feel healthy about eating them. You can't have too much cinnamon in these as far as I'm concerned.

MAKES 12–14 ROLLS

1/2 cup buttermilk

1 (1/4-ounce) package instant dry yeast

1 tablespoon sugar

2 cups bread flour, divided

5 tablespoons unsalted butter, at room temperature, divided

1 1/4 cups firmly packed brown sugar, divided

1/2 teaspoon salt

1 large egg

1 heaping tablespoon cinnamon

1/2 cup golden raisins

1/2 cup powdered sugar

1/8 teaspoon vanilla

1–2 tablespoons cold water

Warm the buttermilk in a saucepan on low heat just until luke-warm. Do not overheat or the buttermilk may curdle. Remove the pan from the heat and stir in the yeast and sugar until both are dissolved and the mixture is frothy. Pour the mixture into the bowl of a stand mixer and stir in 1/2 cup of the flour. Cover the bowl with a tea towel and let the dough rise in a warm, draft-free spot for 45 minutes, or until it is bubbly and looks like a sponge.

Cream 3 tablespoons of the butter with ½ cup of the brown sugar. In a separate bowl, sift together the remaining 1½ cups of flour with the salt. Add the butter and the flour mixtures to the buttermilk mixture along with the egg. Using the dough hook of the stand mixer, beat the dough on medium speed for about 3 minutes, or until it comes together. Place the bowl with the dough in a shallow baking pan containing some hot tap water, cover the bowl with a light tea towel, and place it in a warm, draft-free spot. Let the dough rise for 1 hour, or until approximately doubled in size.

Turn the dough out onto a floured surface. Lightly flour your hands and pat the dough into a rectangle about ½-inch thick. Or you can roll it out if you're adept with a rolling pin. In a small bowl, cream together the remaining ¾ cup of brown sugar and 2 tablespoons of butter and the cinnamon with a spoon or an electric mixer. Sprinkle the cinnamon mixture evenly over the dough. Sprinkle the raisins evenly on top of the cinnamon mixture. Beginning with the long side of the rectangle, roll the dough up jelly-roll style. Cut the roll into ½-inch slices. Place the slices on a nonstick baking sheet or well-greased baking pan, leaving at least 1 inch between slices. Cover the pan with a tea towel and let the rolls rise in a warm, draft-free spot for 30 minutes.

Preheat the oven to 375°. Bake the rolls for 12–15 minutes, or until golden brown. While the rolls are baking, mix together the powdered sugar and vanilla with 1 or 2 tablespoons cold water, just enough to make a spreadable glaze. Drizzle the glaze over the rolls when they are done.

Buttermilk Doughnut Holes

My friend Mary Turner in Chapel Hill, North Carolina, loves doughnuts, and she shared her recipe with me. I made some changes. Rolling out the dough and cutting it to make full-sized doughnuts, like Mary does, seems like too much trouble to me, so I use a cookie scoop to make doughnut holes. I prefer the sweeter flavor of mace to nutmeg.

MAKES 2–4 DOZEN DOUGHNUT HOLES,
depending on the size you make them

---

1 cup sugar
2 large eggs
1 teaspoon baking soda
1 cup buttermilk
3 tablespoons melted unsalted butter
1 tablespoon vanilla
1 teaspoon baking powder
$\frac{1}{2}$ teaspoon mace or nutmeg
$\frac{1}{4}$ teaspoon cinnamon
$3\frac{1}{2}$ cups all-purpose flour
About 6 cups vegetable oil
Powdered sugar

Using a stand mixer, beat together the sugar and eggs until well mixed. Add the baking soda, buttermilk, melted butter, and vanilla, then stir to blend. In a separate bowl, sift together the baking powder, mace or nutmeg, cinnamon, and flour, then stir the mixture into the buttermilk mixture. Cover the bowl tightly and refrigerate the dough overnight.

The next day, in a deep Dutch oven or deep-fat fryer, heat the oil to 370°. Use an instant-read thermometer to monitor the temperature. While the oil heats, spread a piece of wax paper on the counter and lightly flour it. Use a cookie scoop or two spoons to scoop out rounds of dough and place them on the floured wax paper. Only scoop enough dough for one batch, then refrigerate the remaining dough until you are ready to do the next batch. The dough becomes very sticky when it gets warm.

Using a long-handled metal spatula or slotted spoon, place the doughnuts in the oil. Fry them, turning with your spatula, for 1–2 minutes per side, or until they are golden brown on all sides. Watch them carefully; they turn dark quickly. Lower the heat if they seem to be cooking too fast. After draining the doughnuts on paper towels, sprinkle them with powdered sugar and serve warm.

Time for Dinner

MAIN DISHES, SIDE DISHES, SOUPS, AND MORE

Buttermilk brings good things to lunch
and dinner in main dishes, side dishes, hearty
breads, and soups.

Fiery Fried Chicken

If you don't soak chicken in buttermilk before you fry it, why on Earth not? Buttermilk tenderizes the meat, helps ensure a good coating, and adds flavor. Pump it up by adding heat to the soak and the coating. But I have to warn you: You'll be spoiled. Once you fry your own chicken, you'll never be happy with a bucket of bird again.

MAKES 4–6 SERVINGS

1 whole chicken, cut up, or 8 of your favorite chicken pieces
1 quart buttermilk
1 tablespoon hot pepper sauce, such as Tabasco
Vegetable oil
2 cups all-purpose flour
1 teaspoon chili powder
½ teaspoon cayenne (optional, if you like it hotter)
½ teaspoon salt

Place the chicken in a large bowl with a lid or a large reclosable plastic bag. In another bowl, stir together the buttermilk and hot pepper sauce. Pour the buttermilk mixture over the chicken, making sure all the pieces are covered. Cover and refrigerate for 8 hours or overnight.

When ready to cook the chicken, pour enough vegetable oil into an electric frying pan or heavy frying pan to come to a depth of about 2 inches. Heat on medium-high heat to 350°.

Drain the chicken but do not rinse it. Combine the flour, chili powder, cayenne (if using), and salt in a large reclosable plastic bag. Put 3 or 4 pieces of chicken into the bag and shake to coat them. Shake off the excess flour when you remove the pieces. Place the pieces in the hot oil but do not crowd them. Adjust the heat to keep the oil temperature at 325°–350°. You may cover the pan briefly to keep down spatters, but do not cook the chicken completely with the pan covered or the crust will be soggy.

Fry the pieces for 5–8 minutes, or until the undersides are brown. Turn with tongs and cook another 5–8 minutes, adjusting the heat if the pieces are browning too quickly. The chicken is done when the internal temperature is 180° on an instant-read thermometer or when no pink juices run out when the meat is pricked with a sharp knife.

Drain the pieces on wire racks set over plates before serving.

Marinated Curry Chicken

Traditional Indian tandoori chicken uses a yogurt marinade. My buttermilk version is easy enough to make even a weeknight dinner exotic. The acid in buttermilk makes meats as tender as magnolia petals.

MAKES 6 SERVINGS

2 cups buttermilk
1 tablespoon hot Madras curry powder
1 teaspoon turmeric
4 garlic cloves, crushed
$\frac{1}{2}$ teaspoon salt
1 small onion, sliced
6 boneless chicken breast halves
Olive oil
Chutney (optional)

In a medium bowl, whisk together the buttermilk, curry powder, turmeric, garlic, salt, and onion until combined. Place the chicken in a reclosable plastic bag, then pour the buttermilk mixture over it. Turn the bag to be sure all the chicken is covered, then refrigerate for 12 hours.

Preheat the oven to 350°. Remove the chicken, onion, and garlic from the marinade and place them in a nonstick baking dish. Drizzle with olive oil, cover, and bake for 45 minutes, or until no pink juices emerge when the chicken is pierced with a sharp knife. Serve with your favorite chutney, if desired.

Faux Fryers

There are some people who want the flavor of fried chicken without the shower of oil that can cover your kitchen when making it. The problem I've found with most baked "fried" chicken is that it lacks crispness. The solution: crunchy cornflakes. This recipe is from my cookbook Wings: More Than 50 High-Flying Recipes for America's Favorite Snack *(John Wiley & Sons, 2009). You can use larger chicken pieces, but allow a longer soak in the buttermilk (closer to overnight) and possibly a longer cooking time.*

MAKES 24 PIECES

12 wings, cut in half at the joints, wing tips removed
   and discarded
2 cups buttermilk
5 cups coarsely crushed unsweetened cornflakes
4 teaspoons dried thyme
2 teaspoons dried basil
1 teaspoon salt
1 teaspoon black pepper

Place the wings in a reclosable plastic bag and pour in the buttermilk. Refrigerate for 2–3 hours.

Preheat the oven to 400°. Cover a rimmed baking sheet with foil and spray the foil with nonstick cooking spray.

Drain the wings but do not rinse them. In a large bowl, combine the crushed cornflakes, thyme, basil, salt, and pepper. Roll the wings in the mixture, pressing the coating in lightly. Place the wings on the baking sheet. Bake for 40–50 minutes, or until done.

Martha's Pan-Fried Soft-Shell Crabs

My friend Martha Waggoner in Raleigh, North Carolina, was waiting in line at a pharmacy and got to talking to the guy behind her. Turns out he was a chef, and he gave her the crucial part of this technique for cooking her favorite seafood: soaking the crabs in buttermilk. "I don't know what it does," Martha says, "but they turn out really tender." It's the witchcraft of buttermilk, Martha.

MAKES 2 MAIN-DISH OR 4 APPETIZER SERVINGS

---

4 soft-shell crabs
About 2 cups buttermilk, or just enough to cover the crabs
A few shakes of hot pepper sauce, such as Tabasco
All-purpose flour seasoned with salt and black pepper
3 tablespoons unsalted butter

Place the soft-shell crabs in a shallow dish. In a bowl, stir together the buttermilk and hot pepper sauce. Pour the combination over the crabs and let sit for about 5 minutes. Place the seasoned flour in another shallow dish. Remove the crabs from the buttermilk. Don't rinse them, but let the excess buttermilk drip off. Dredge the crabs in the seasoned flour.

Place a frying pan over medium heat and add the butter. When the butter has melted, slip in the crabs. Fry them for a few minutes until the undersides are lightly browned, then turn them over and fry the other side. Serve warm.

Buttermilk-Poached Fish with Cilantro-Lime Butter

Cooking fish this way is a revelation. The fish comes out very tender and sweet, and if you're one of those people who don't like "fishy tasting" fish, this method is for you. It even makes frozen fish taste better. Another buttermilk miracle.

MAKES 4 SERVINGS

4 6-ounce fillets of fish such as tilapia, snapper,
   flounder, trout, or perch
Salt and black pepper
3–4 cups buttermilk
6 tablespoons unsalted butter
½ cup chopped onion
2 cloves garlic, chopped
1 cup chopped cilantro
Juice of 2 limes

Place the fish fillets in a saucepan or Dutch oven large enough to hold them in a single layer and sprinkle with salt and pepper. Pour in enough buttermilk to just cover the fish. Place the pan over medium heat and bring the liquid to a gentle simmer. Simmer the fish for 2 minutes, then use a spatula to turn over the fillets and cook for another minute, or until the fish is cooked through and flakes easily. Remove the fish from the pan with a slotted spatula and keep warm.

Place the butter in a sauté pan over medium heat. Add the onion and garlic. Stir and cook for a few minutes, until the onion and garlic are soft but not brown. Remove the pan from the heat, then stir in the cilantro and lime juice. Pour the butter mixture over the fish and serve immediately.

Blossom's Buttermilk Fried Calamari with Red Pepper Remoulade

Adam Close, the executive chef at Blossom Restaurant in Charleston, South Carolina, believes that cooking with buttermilk is a southern tradition. This dish is one of the most popular on the menu.

MAKES 4 SERVINGS

FOR THE RED PEPPER REMOULADE

1 red bell pepper, seeds and ribs removed
1/4 cup chopped parsley
4 green onions, chopped
Juice of 1 lemon
1 tablespoon Worcestershire sauce
1 cup mayonnaise

FOR THE CALAMARI

1 pound squid (rings only)
1 cup buttermilk
3 cups all-purpose flour
1 tablespoon garlic powder
1/2 teaspoon paprika
1/2 tablespoon white pepper
2 tablespoons kosher salt
1 gallon peanut oil
Lemon wedges, for serving

To prepare the Red Pepper Remoulade, combine all the ingredients in a blender and purée until smooth. Cover and refrigerate. The remoulade may be made a few hours ahead.

To prepare the calamari, rinse the squid, drain well, and pat dry with a paper towel. In a stainless steel bowl, combine the squid and the buttermilk and let it marinate in the refrigerator overnight.

When ready to cook, combine the flour, garlic powder, paprika, white pepper, and salt. Remove the squid from the buttermilk and add it to the seasoned flour, tossing to coat well. Make sure all the moisture is absorbed by the flour.

Put the oil in a pot large enough to contain it with plenty of room to spare. Heat the oil over medium heat to 350°. Use a thermometer to monitor the temperature, keeping in mind that the calamari will somewhat cool the oil once it is added.

Shake off the excess flour from the calamari and add it to the hot oil. Cook for 30 seconds, being careful not to overcook it, then remove with a slotted spoon. Place the calamari carefully on a plate lined with a paper towel to absorb any excess oil. Serve with lemon wedges and Red Pepper Remoulade.

Sundried Tomato and Parmesan Quiche

This quiche makes a quick lunch or brunch dish. Buttermilk adds a special flavor that regular milk lacks.

MAKES 1 9-INCH QUICHE

1 9-inch piecrust, unbaked
1 cup chopped sundried tomatoes
½ cup grated Parmesan cheese
1 tablespoon chopped fresh basil
¾ cup buttermilk
¾ cup milk
4 large eggs
2 tablespoons all-purpose flour
½ teaspoon salt
½ teaspoon black pepper

Preheat the oven to 375°. Line a 9-inch quiche pan or pie pan with the crust. Sprinkle the sundried tomatoes, Parmesan, and basil evenly over the crust.

In a medium-sized bowl, whisk together the buttermilk, milk, eggs, and flour until smooth. Stir in the salt and pepper. Pour the buttermilk mixture into the piecrust. Bake for 30 minutes, or until the filling is set.

Potato Salad with Buttermilk-Chive Dressing

I wrote an entire cookbook on potato salad, but I found that I lacked one recipe. Buttermilk inspired this brand-new recipe.

MAKES 6 SERVINGS

1 cup buttermilk
1/4 cup mayonnaise
2 teaspoons Dijon mustard
2 teaspoons prepared horseradish
2 tablespoons chopped fresh chives
1 tablespoon chopped fresh parsley
1/4 teaspoon garlic powder
1/4 teaspoon salt
1/2 teaspoon black pepper
3 pounds yellow potatoes
3/4 cup chopped celery
1/4 cup dill pickle cubes, drained

In a large bowl, whisk together the buttermilk, mayonnaise, mustard, and horseradish until smooth. Stir in the chives, parsley, garlic powder, salt, and pepper. You can refrigerate the dressing overnight, if you like.

Cook the potatoes in boiling water until a sharp knife passes easily into them. Drain and let cool until you can handle them, then peel them and cut them into chunks. In a large bowl, toss the potatoes with the celery and dill pickle cubes. Pour on the dressing and toss to combine. Refrigerate, covered, for several hours. Serve chilled.

Creamy Vegetable Mash

Enough butter and cream will make any mashed potatoes good. But it takes real talent to make cauliflower and parsnips into a side dish that usurps potatoes' spot at the table. Buttermilk is the star.

MAKES 4–6 SERVINGS

½ pound parsnips
1 head cauliflower
3 cloves garlic, peeled
3 tablespoons unsalted butter
¾ cup buttermilk
½ cup grated Parmesan cheese
Salt and black pepper to taste
2 tablespoons chopped fresh chives

Bring a large pot of water to boil while you peel the parsnips and cut them into small chunks. Cut the cauliflower into florets. When the water comes to a boil, put in the parsnips, cauliflower, and garlic. Boil for about 10 minutes or until all the vegetables are very soft. Take them out at different times, if necessary. Drain well.

Put the drained, but still warm, vegetables into a large bowl or the bowl of a stand mixer. Use a potato masher or the mixer's paddle attachment to thoroughly work in the butter, then add the buttermilk. Mash or beat until the mixture is very smooth. Stir in the Parmesan. Taste, then add salt and pepper (a lot of pepper is good, I think). Using a spatula, stir in the chives. Serve warm.

Indian-Style Green Rice

Asian rice dishes often include coconut milk. I wondered what would happen if I created a version using buttermilk. Good things, that's what happened. Add more serrano pepper if you like things hot. You could even throw in some spinach or peas if you don't have a pea-hating husband like I do.

MAKES 6 SERVINGS

1 teaspoon olive oil

1/2 cup chopped green onions

1 serrano pepper, seeded and chopped

1 cup raw basmati rice

1 1/2 teaspoons finely chopped fresh ginger

1/2 teaspoon garam masala

3/4 teaspoon salt

1/2 cup buttermilk

1/2 cup chopped cilantro

1/2 cup chopped mint

Place the olive oil in a small sauté pan over medium heat. Add the green onions and serrano pepper and cook for a few minutes, until soft but not brown.

Put the rice and 2 cups of water in a medium-sized saucepan. Bring to a boil, then stir in the ginger, garam masala, and salt, plus the contents of the sauté pan. Cover, reduce the heat to a simmer, and cook for 20 minutes, or until the rice is done.

Empty the rice mixture into a bowl and let it cool for a few minutes, tossing occasionally with a spoon. When it has cooled slightly, stir in the buttermilk, cilantro, and mint.

Don't-Fear-the-Slime Okra

*I am so tired of hearing the same old gripe from okra-phobes —
slime, slime, slime. Fine, y'all. I defy you to find a drop of slime in
this crispy, buttermilk-dipped okra.*

MAKES 4–6 SERVINGS

1 pound small okra pods
2½ cups buttermilk
1 cup white or yellow cornmeal
1 cup all-purpose flour
½ teaspoon chili powder
½ teaspoon salt
½ teaspoon black pepper
About 2 cups vegetable oil
518 West's Buttermilk Dressing (page 78), for dipping
    (optional)

Rinse the okra pods and cut off any long stems, but leave the
pods whole. Pour the buttermilk into a bowl. In a shallow pan
(a pie pan is good), stir together the cornmeal, flour, chili powder, salt, and pepper.

Pour enough oil in a frying pan to come to a depth of about
1 inch. Place over medium heat.

Get ready to fry. Line up your ingredients like this: okra,
buttermilk, flour mixture. Dip the okra in the buttermilk, let
the excess drain off, then roll in the flour mixture and gently tap
off any excess. Place the pods in the hot oil and fry until golden
brown. Don't turn them too often or you may knock off the
crunchy crust.

Let the okra drain on paper towels and sprinkle with additional salt, if needed. Serve as is or with 518 West's Buttermilk
Dressing as a dip.

Tex-Mex Corn Pudding

Can it be a southern Thanksgiving without corn pudding on the table? Classic corn pudding is a creamy, mild blend, but sometimes tradition needs a little kick in the kernels. Sit this version next to the bird and get everyone talking.

MAKES 6–8 SERVINGS

---

3 cups corn kernels (fresh or frozen, no need to thaw)
¾ cup yellow cornmeal
½ cup grated cheddar cheese
½ cup canned chopped green chilies, drained
4 green onions, chopped
½ teaspoon salt
½ teaspoon baking soda
3 large eggs
1½ cups buttermilk
½ teaspoon chili powder

Preheat the oven to 350°. Spray a 1½ to 2-quart baking dish with nonstick cooking spray.

In a large bowl, stir together all the ingredients. Pour the mixture into the prepared dish. Bake for 45–50 minutes or until lightly browned on top.

Jazzed-Up Cornbread

The best kind of cornbread is the kind your mother made, but here's my frisky version. Every good cornbread starts with buttermilk and should be cooked in a heated cast-iron frying pan to achieve the crispy exterior that contrasts with the fluffy interior. My pan is more than fifty years old — my mother received it as a wedding present — and is as nonstick as Teflon after decades of seasoning. Use good-quality, stone-ground cornmeal. I like to purchase mine locally.

MAKES 6–8 SERVINGS

---

2 tablespoons unsalted butter plus 3 tablespoons melted
   unsalted butter, divided
1 cup all-purpose flour
1 cup stone-ground cornmeal
½ teaspoon salt
2 teaspoons baking powder
½ teaspoon baking soda
½ teaspoon chili powder
1 cup buttermilk
1 (8.25-ounce) can creamed corn or ½ cup frozen corn,
   thawed and drained
1 tablespoon canned chopped green chilies, well drained
1 tablespoon sugar
1 large egg

Preheat the oven to 350°. Place a cast-iron frying pan in the oven to get superhot. When the pan is hot, add the 2 tablespoons of butter and swirl it around to coat the pan.

In a large bowl, combine the flour, cornmeal, salt, baking powder, baking soda, and chili powder. In another large bowl, combine the buttermilk, corn, chilies, sugar, egg, and 3 tablespoons melted butter. Stir until well mixed. Pour the wet mixture into the dry mixture and stir only until combined and no lumps remain. Don't overmix. Pour the batter into the hot pan.

Bake for 30–45 minutes, or until a toothpick inserted into the center comes out clean. Serve warm straight from the pan.

Fried Cornbread

Where I grew up in western North Carolina, we baked our cornbread. But friends from the eastern part of the state praise fried cornbread. Luckily, the construction guys working on my house the day I tested this recipe were from eastern North Carolina, and they compared mine in detail to the kind their grandmothers made. I think these patties would make an interesting base for a southern-style eggs Benedict.

MAKES 10–12 PATTIES

1½ cups yellow or white cornmeal
½ cup all-purpose flour
2 teaspoons baking powder
¼ teaspoon sugar
¾ teaspoon salt
1½ cups buttermilk
½ cup corn kernels (fresh or frozen, thawed, and drained)
About 2 cups vegetable oil

In a large bowl, stir together the cornmeal, flour, baking powder, sugar, and salt. Stir in the buttermilk, then the corn.

Heat the oil in a large sauté pan over medium heat. Scoop out about 2 tablespoons of the batter for each patty and place it in the hot oil, pressing gently to spread it out to about a ¼-inch thickness. Don't make the patties too thick or they will not cook all the way through. Don't crowd the pan, and adjust the heat if they seem to be cooking too quickly. Fry the patties for about 2 minutes or until brown, then flip them and cook the other side. Drain on paper towels. Serve warm.

Rochelle's Vidalia Hushpuppies

The guest of honor at the pig-picking had emerged from a brine in the host's bathtub and was perfuming the yard around the cooker when I met Rochelle Myers from Harpers Ferry, West Virginia. She was standing over a pot of hot oil in which floated light pillows of cornmeal. Rochelle, chef-owner of Rochelle Myers Catering and Cooking Classes and a freelance food writer for the Frederick (Maryland) News-Post, *was kind enough to share her recipe with me.*

MAKES 3–4 DOZEN HUSHPUPPIES

3 cups self-rising white cornmeal
1 cup all-purpose flour
1 teaspoon baking powder
1 small Vidalia onion, diced
1 tablespoon sugar
2 cups buttermilk
2 tablespoons rendered bacon fat
Vegetable oil
Sea salt

In a large bowl, combine the cornmeal, flour, baking powder, onion, and sugar. Form a well in the center. In a separate bowl, combine the buttermilk and bacon fat. Pour the buttermilk mixture into the well. Stir until the dry ingredients are just moistened.

Heat a deep-fat fryer or large pot of vegetable oil to 340°. Drop the batter into the oil from a large spoon, or scoop the batter using a cookie scoop or ice cream scoop. Fry the dough for about 1½ minutes per side, turning when golden brown.

Remove the hushpuppies from the fryer and drain on paper towels. Sprinkle with salt and serve hot.

Buttermilk Herb Rolls

The texture of these light rolls and the herb fragrance are irresistible. My tasters said, "Awesome! Do not even need butter!" and suggested using leftover rolls as a base for chicken pot pie.

MAKES ABOUT 30 ROLLS

---

1 (¼-ounce) package instant dry yeast

2 tablespoons sugar, divided

¼ cup warm water

1 cup buttermilk

¼ cup plus about 2 tablespoons melted unsalted butter, divided

3 cups bread flour

½ teaspoon baking soda

1½ teaspoons salt

1 tablespoon dried dill weed

1 teaspoon dried thyme

Stir together the yeast and 1 tablespoon of the sugar in the warm water. Let sit until frothy.

In a small saucepan over low heat, warm the buttermilk just until it feels warm when you dip in a finger. Do not overheat the buttermilk or it may curdle. When the buttermilk is lukewarm, remove it from the heat and stir in ¼ cup of the melted butter. Add the buttermilk mixture to the yeast and stir together gently with a fork.

Sift together the flour, baking soda, salt, and remaining 1 tablespoon of sugar into a large bowl. Gently stir in the herbs. Pour the buttermilk-yeast mixture into the dry ingredients and stir together with a large spoon. By hand or using the dough hook of a stand mixer, beat the dough for 3–4 minutes, until it is soft and smooth but not spongy.

Place the bowl in a shallow baking pan containing hot tap water, cover it with a light tea towel, and place it in a warm, draft-free spot. Let the dough rise for 1 hour, or until approximately doubled in size.

When the dough has risen, punch it down. Spray a rimmed baking pan with nonstick cooking spray. Pull off a piece of the dough about the size of a ping-pong ball, dip it in the remaining 2 tablespoons of melted butter, and place it in the baking pan. Repeat with the remaining dough. Leave enough space between the rolls for the dough to rise, about a couple of inches. Do not overhandle the rolls, just pinch, tuck under the rough end, and dip in butter. Cover the baking pan with a light tea towel, place it in a warm, draft-free spot, and let the rolls rise until doubled in size, about 1 hour.

Preheat the oven to 400°. Bake the rolls for about 18 minutes or until golden brown.

Cool Cucumber Soup

Cool cucumbers and icy buttermilk—what a way to chill out on a fiery summer day. This is a great do-ahead soup for a summer dinner party.

MAKES ABOUT 4 1-CUP SERVINGS

4 large cucumbers
4 green onions
2½ cups buttermilk
¾ teaspoon salt, or to taste
2 teaspoons chopped fresh dill

Peel the cucumbers, remove and discard the seeds, and cut them into chunks. Cut the green onions into chunks, using the green and white portions. Put the cucumbers and green onions into a food processor and process the vegetables to a coarse purée.

Add the buttermilk, salt, and dill. Process until the soup is smooth. Taste and add more salt, if needed.

Chill the soup for 3–4 hours. Serve cold in chilled bowls or shot glasses.

Butternut Squash Soup

A whole butternut squash can be a hard nut to crack, but with a sharp knife and a steady surface, you can do it. Or you can find already cut-up chunks of butternut squash in supermarket produce sections, which makes this soup even easier to prepare. Boil or roast the squash as you prefer.

MAKES ABOUT 4 1-CUP SERVINGS

2 tablespoons unsalted butter

$1\frac{1}{2}$ cups chopped onion

1 tablespoon chopped fresh ginger

1 cup water

1 stalk lemongrass (about 3 inches), split lengthwise
and lightly crushed

2 cups mashed cooked butternut squash

2 cups buttermilk

$\frac{1}{2}$ teaspoon salt, or to taste, if needed

Chopped cilantro, for garnish

Place a large sauté pan over medium heat and add the butter. When the butter is melted, add the onion and ginger. Stir and cook for a few minutes, just until the onion is soft. Add the water and lemongrass, raise the heat to medium-high, and simmer 5–6 minutes, until the water is mostly gone. Remove the pan from the heat and let cool to room temperature.

When the mixture is cool, use tongs to remove the lemongrass pieces and discard them. Place the onion mixture and the butternut squash in a blender with the buttermilk and purée until smooth. Taste and add salt, if needed.

Chill for several hours and serve cold. Add a little water if the soup thickens while chilling. Sprinkle each serving with cilantro.

Roasted Red Bell Pepper Soup

I love the color of this soup. It's especially nice when the summer tomatoes, peppers, and basil are flooding in and I'm looking for different ways to use them.

MAKES 4–6 SERVINGS

1 tablespoon unsalted butter
½ cup chopped onion
2 cloves garlic, chopped
½ cup chicken broth
2 roasted red bell peppers, seeds removed, coarsely chopped
1¼ cups buttermilk
1 small tomato, peeled and chopped
1 teaspoon salt
1 teaspoon black pepper
1½ teaspoons sugar
2 teaspoons chopped fresh basil

Heat the butter in a sauté pan over medium heat. Add the onion and garlic and cook until soft, just a few minutes. Remove from the heat.

Place the chicken broth, roasted red bell peppers, buttermilk, tomato, salt, pepper, and sugar in a blender along with the cooked onion and garlic and purée until smooth. Stir in the basil, cover, and refrigerate for several hours. Serve cold.

Sweet Endings

PIES, CAKES, ICE CREAMS, AND OTHER DELIGHTS

Desserts with the zing of buttermilk are sweets with a difference. Try classic pies, rich cakes, silky panna cotta, or refreshing ice creams.

Sweet Tea Buttermilk Pie

Few things are more southern than buttermilk and sweet iced tea, so I immediately thought of combining them in a classic pie. The tea gives a subtle flavor to this custardy pie.

MAKES 1 9-INCH PIE

1 cup buttermilk
1 tablespoon loose black tea leaves
1 9-inch piecrust, unbaked
$\frac{1}{2}$ teaspoon grated lemon zest
$\frac{3}{4}$ cup sugar
2 tablespoons all-purpose flour
2 large eggs
$\frac{1}{4}$ teaspoon vanilla
4 tablespoons melted unsalted butter
Fresh mint leaves, for garnish

Warm the buttermilk in a small saucepan over medium-low heat just until it begins to steam. Do not allow it to boil or it may curdle. Remove the pan from the heat and stir in the tea leaves. Let it sit for 1 hour, then strain out the tea leaves and reserve the infused buttermilk.

Line a 9-inch pie pan with the crust. Preheat the oven to 425°.

Use a fork or whisk to combine the lemon zest, sugar, and flour in a large bowl. In another bowl, whisk together the eggs, vanilla, infused buttermilk, and melted butter. Add the buttermilk mixture to the flour mixture and whisk to combine well.

Pour the filling into the crust. Bake for 10 minutes, then reduce the heat to 350° and bake until the edges puff and the center is no longer liquid, about 30 more minutes. If the crust begins to overbrown before the center is set, reduce the heat to 300°. Cool to room temperature on a wire rack. Garnish the pie with mint leaves before serving.

Sweet Potato Pie with Ginger and Orange

Sweet potato pie for Thanksgiving is a southern tradition, but many sweet potato pies simply echo the flavors of pumpkin pie. I decided to make something different by using buttermilk, fresh ginger, and sweet orange. You can either boil or roast the sweet potatoes. I like to roast them because I think it adds a richer flavor.

MAKES 1 9-INCH PIE

1 9-inch piecrust, unbaked
1 cup firmly packed brown sugar
1 teaspoon finely grated fresh ginger
1½ teaspoons finely grated orange zest
¼ teaspoon salt
1 cup buttermilk
1½ cups mashed cooked sweet potato
2 large eggs
2 tablespoons melted unsalted butter

Preheat the oven to 350°. Line a 9-inch pie pan with the crust.

In a large bowl, whisk together the sugar, ginger, orange zest, and salt until combined and no lumps remain. Add the buttermilk, sweet potato, eggs, and melted butter. Use an electric mixer to blend all the ingredients until the mixture is smooth.

Pour the mixture into the piecrust. Bake for 50–55 minutes, or until the edges have puffed up slightly and the center does not feel liquid when tapped lightly with a finger.

18 Seaboard's Buttermilk Pie with Riesling-Marinated Peaches

I was pondering a classic buttermilk pie recipe when I had dinner at 18 Seaboard in Raleigh, North Carolina, where chef Jason Smith is committed to local ingredients. This pie was so much better than anything I'd come up with that I begged for the recipe, and pastry chef Billy Apperson was glad to provide it. The fruit topping varies with the season. Freeze the extra piecrusts — you'll be wanting more of this pie.

MAKES 1 9-INCH PIE

FOR THE RIESLING-MARINATED PEACHES
1 pint peaches, peeled and sliced
1/2 cup Riesling (see Note below)
1/2 cup simple syrup (see Note below)

FOR THE PIECRUST
3 cups all-purpose flour
1/3 cup sugar
1 cup chilled unsalted butter, cut into 1/2-inch pieces
2 large egg yolks
1/3 cup milk

FOR THE FILLING
9 tablespoons unsalted butter, at room temperature
1 1/2 cups sugar, divided
3 large eggs, separated
4 1/2 tablespoons all-purpose flour
1 1/2 tablespoons lemon juice
1 1/2 cups buttermilk

To prepare the Riesling-Marinated Peaches, place the peaches in a nonreactive container with a lid or a reclosable plastic bag. Pour the Riesling and simple syrup over the peaches. Cover and refrigerate for 24 hours.

To prepare the piecrust, in a food processor, combine the flour and sugar. Add the butter and pulse until the pieces are about half the size of a green pea. Add the egg yolks and milk and process just until the crust has a crumbly texture. Do not overprocess or the crust will be tough. Divide the dough into 3 balls of equal size. Wrap each ball tightly in plastic wrap.

Place two of the wrapped dough balls in a reclosable plastic bag or other airtight container. Refrigerate or freeze for later use. (Dough will keep for up to a week in the refrigerator or up to a month in the freezer.) Refrigerate the third dough ball for 30 minutes.

Preheat the oven to 350°. Roll out the refrigerated dough on a floured surface to a thickness of about ¼ inch. Transfer to a 9-inch pie pan and place in the freezer for 15 minutes.

Cut a piece of parchment paper a little larger than the pie plate and place it on top of the crust. Fill the parchment-lined piecrust with pie weights (dried beans or coffee beans will also work). Bake for 10 minutes. Rotate the piecrust 180° (to ensure even browning) and bake for 5 more minutes.

Take the crust out of the oven and reduce the temperature to 325°. Carefully remove the parchment paper and pie weights and return the crust to the oven. Bake for another 5 minutes, or until the crust is cooked through.

To prepare the filling, with an electric mixer, cream the butter and 1 cup of the sugar. Add the egg yolks one at a time. After the egg yolks are thoroughly incorporated, mix in the flour, lemon juice, and buttermilk.

In a separate bowl with clean beaters, beat the egg whites with the remaining ½ cup sugar until soft peaks form. Fold this mixture into the buttermilk mixture. Pour into the baked piecrust and bake at 325° for 30 minutes. Rotate the pie 180° and bake for 20–30 more minutes, or until the filling is set (the center will still be slightly jiggly) and the top is golden brown. Cool to room temperature on a wire rack before serving with Riesling-Marinated Peaches.

NOTE ❋ Billy Apperson likes to use a North Carolina–produced Riesling from Shelton Vineyards.

Simple syrup is made from equal parts water and sugar—for this recipe, that's ½ cup water and ½ cup sugar. Combine both in a saucepan and bring to a boil, stirring, until the sugar is dissolved. Let the syrup cool before using it. It can be refrigerated for use in drinks and desserts.

Summer Blueberry Cobbler

There's nothing wrong with fancy cobblers topped by sweet biscuits. But when the blueberries are in season at the farmers' market, I want to get them into a dessert and onto my table as quickly as I can. This is the easiest cobbler ever. My mother and grandmother made it with "sweet milk," but buttermilk gives the cake part of the cobbler extra richness.

MAKES 6 SERVINGS

6 tablespoons unsalted butter
1 cup all-purpose flour
¾ cup sugar
1½ teaspoons baking powder
¼ teaspoon salt
1 cup buttermilk
1 large egg
½ teaspoon vanilla
2 cups fresh blueberries (or frozen, thawed, and drained)

Preheat the oven to 375°. Place the butter in an 8 × 8-inch baking dish and put it in the oven until the butter is melted. Do not allow the butter to burn.

In a large bowl, mix together the flour, sugar, baking powder, and salt. Add the buttermilk, egg, and vanilla. Stir until the batter is smooth.

Pour the batter into the baking dish, over the melted butter. Spoon the blueberries evenly over the batter. Bake for 30–40 minutes, or until golden brown.

Jan's Buttermilk Pound Cake

My friend Jan Norris in West Palm Beach, Florida, got this recipe from her mother. Jan says her mom carried this cake to every family event she can remember. Jan is a busy woman, running Jan-Norris.com and writing about food, but she continues the tradition and keeps a cake or two in her freezer at all times. She says leftovers (if there are any) are great for breakfast, toasted with a little jam.

MAKES ABOUT 20 SERVINGS

1 cup unsalted butter, at room temperature

3 cups sugar

5 extra-large eggs or 6 large eggs

$\frac{1}{2}$ teaspoon baking soda

$\frac{1}{2}$ teaspoon salt

3 cups all-purpose flour

1 cup buttermilk

1 teaspoon vanilla extract

FOR THE GLAZE (OPTIONAL)

$1\frac{1}{2}$ cups powdered sugar

Juice of 1 lemon or lime

Grated lemon or lime zest

Prepare a 10-inch tube pan by coating the inner surface with nonstick cooking spray or vegetable oil and dusting it with flour. Preheat the oven to 325°.

Place the butter and sugar in the bowl of a stand mixer. Beat on high speed until creamy and pale, about 5 minutes. Break the eggs into a small bowl and whisk gently to break the yolks. Add the eggs to the butter mixture in two additions, beating well after each and scraping the sides of the bowl between beatings.

In a medium bowl, whisk together the baking soda, salt, and flour. On medium speed, beat ⅓ of the flour mixture into the creamed butter mixture. Stop the mixer and add half of the buttermilk. Turn the mixer on low to prevent spatters and beat for 30 seconds, then switch to high speed and beat for 1 minute. Add another ⅓ of the flour mixture, the rest of the buttermilk, the vanilla, and then the rest of the flour mixture, beating well after each addition and scraping the bowl periodically to incorporate all the ingredients. The batter will be thick.

Scrape the batter into the prepared tube pan and rap the bottom of the pan on the counter to release any air bubbles. Bake in the lower third of the oven for about 1 hour or until a toothpick or cake tester comes out clean. The cake may crack on top, but this is OK.

Cool in the pan on a wire rack for 5 minutes, then turn the cake out onto the rack to continue cooling.

To make the glaze, combine the powdered sugar and lemon or lime juice until smooth, then stir in some grated zest for color. Brush it on the cooled cake.

Magie's Naturally
Red Velvet Cupcakes

These cupcakes caught my eye at the Triangle Food Blogger Bake Sale in Durham, North Carolina, because they weren't overloaded with icing. Even better, the baker, Magie Lanz of Cary, North Carolina, told me she avoids using the typical red food coloring in favor of natural beet juice dye. My tasters said the frosting reminded them of cheesecake.

MAKES 24–30 CUPCAKES

FOR THE BEET JUICE DYE

1 beet, sliced

¼ cup white vinegar

1 cup water

FOR THE CUPCAKES

¾ cup unsalted butter, at room temperature

1¾ cups sugar

5 large egg whites, at room temperature

1½ cups buttermilk, at room temperature

1 teaspoon vanilla

1 cup cake flour

1 cup all-purpose flour

¾ cup nonalkalized cocoa powder (don't use Dutch processed)

1 teaspoon baking soda

1 teaspoon baking powder

1 teaspoon salt

¼ cup beet juice dye

FOR THE FROSTING

12 ounces cream cheese, at room temperature

¾ cup unsalted butter, at room temperature

2 cups powdered sugar

To prepare the beet juice dye, put the beet, vinegar, and water in a saucepan. Place the saucepan over medium heat, bring the liquid to a boil, then reduce the heat and slowly simmer it down until there's about ¼ cup left. Strain out the beet and let the liquid cool before using. The juice will keep up to a month, covered and refrigerated.

To prepare the cupcakes, preheat the oven to 375°. Place paper liners in approximately 30 muffin cups.

Beat the butter and sugar together with an electric mixer or stand mixer until the sugar is dissolved and the texture is light and fluffy. Add the egg whites one at a time. Beat until the texture becomes almost like frosting. Then beat in the buttermilk and vanilla.

In a separate bowl, sift together the flours, cocoa, baking soda, baking powder, and salt. Gradually beat the dry ingredients into the wet ingredients until the batter is smooth. The texture and consistency should be something like chocolate mousse. Stir in the beet juice dye.

Spoon the cupcake batter into the muffin pans. Bake for 15–20 minutes, or until a toothpick inserted into the center of 1 cupcake comes out clean. Do not overbake. Let the cupcakes cool to room temperature on a wire rack before frosting.

To prepare the frosting, using an electric mixer, beat the cream cheese, butter, and sugar together until smooth and fluffy. Put the frosting in a quart-size reclosable plastic bag, cut off a corner, and pipe spirals of frosting onto each cupcake. Keep the frosted cupcakes refrigerated, tightly covered, until serving.

Janice's Buttermilk Cookies

Janice McLaughlin of Raleigh, North Carolina, got this recipe from her grandmother, Marie Mercedes Comeau McLaughlin, who was from the French-speaking part of Nova Scotia. These soft, sweet cookies are similar to tea cakes and show off buttermilk's flavor subtly.

MAKES ABOUT 5 DOZEN COOKIES

3 large eggs

2 cups sugar

2 cups vegetable shortening

2 cups buttermilk

1 heaping teaspoon baking soda

2 heaping teaspoons nutmeg

1 heaping teaspoon baking powder

1 teaspoon salt

8 cups all-purpose flour

Preheat the oven to 400°. Spray a cookie sheet with nonstick cooking spray.

In the bowl of a stand mixer with the paddle blade, cream the eggs, sugar, and shortening until smooth. In a separate bowl, whisk together the buttermilk and baking soda. Add the buttermilk mixture to the egg mixture and beat until smooth. Stir in the nutmeg, baking powder, salt, and flour. The dough will be soft.

Roll out the dough to a ¼-inch thickness or press it out with floured hands. Cut out the cookies with a biscuit cutter and place them on the prepared baking sheet.

Bake for 8–9 minutes, or until the bottoms of the cookies are lightly browned. Bake in batches. If using more than one cookie sheet in the oven, rotate the sheets to promote even cooking.

Lemongrass–Green Tea Panna Cotta

Anything that translates as "cooked cream" has got to be good. Adding buttermilk brings a tart edge to this dessert's richness. The Asian flavors are my little twist. And green tea is good for you, right?

MAKES 6 SERVINGS

1¼ cups heavy cream
½ cup sugar
1 3-inch piece lemongrass, split lengthwise and lightly crushed
1½ teaspoons green tea leaves
1 package unflavored gelatin
3 tablespoons cold water
1 cup buttermilk
Riesling-Marinated Peaches (page 56), for serving

In a medium saucepan over medium-low heat, combine the cream, sugar, lemongrass, and tea leaves. Stir and heat until the sugar is dissolved. Reduce the heat to very low and let simmer for 10 minutes, stirring occasionally.

In a medium-sized bowl, dissolve the gelatin in the water. Let sit for 5 minutes. Strain the cream mixture to remove the solids, then whisk it into the gelatin while still warm. Let cool until just slightly warm, then gradually whisk in the buttermilk.

Pour the mixture into 6-ounce ramekins, teacups, or other containers. Cover and refrigerate 3–4 hours or until set. To serve, gently run a warm butter knife around the inside of the ramekin or cup and tap the panna cotta onto a plate. Serve with Riesling-Marinated Peaches.

Light Lemon Ice Cream

I don't care if it's 90° or 9° — I love ice cream. The simple, fresh flavor that you get when you combine buttermilk and lemon is refreshing anytime. Because there's no heavy cream in this recipe, you can eat plenty of it with little guilt.

MAKES ABOUT 1 PINT

²/₃ cup sugar
1 tablespoon finely grated lemon zest
2 cups buttermilk

Whisk the sugar and lemon zest into the buttermilk. Chill the mixture for several hours or overnight. Freeze according to your ice cream maker's instructions.

NOTE ✱ This ice cream tastes best when eaten the day it is prepared.

Lavender Ice Cream

*Lavender farms are popping up all over the South, and I am
intrigued with using the herb in cooking. The tangy buttermilk
beautifully balances the floral flavor of the lavender. Look for lavender that is labeled for culinary use and has been grown organi-
cally, without chemical sprays.*

MAKES ABOUT 1 PINT

½ cup heavy cream
1½ cups buttermilk
¾ cup sugar
2 teaspoons dried lavender buds

In a large bowl, whisk together the cream, buttermilk, and
sugar until the sugar is dissolved. Stir in the lavender. Cover
and refrigerate for 12 hours (or longer if you want a stronger
lavender flavor).

Strain out the lavender and discard it. Freeze the cream mixture according to your ice cream maker's instructions.

Chocolate-Hazelnut Ice Cream

The tartness of buttermilk and the sweetness of chocolate — sign me up. This ice cream is so easy to make that you can keep a pint on hand for an emergency or just because it's Tuesday. My tasters said it didn't last twenty-four hours in their houses.

MAKES ABOUT 1½ PINTS

1 cup heavy cream
4 large egg yolks
½ cup chocolate-hazelnut spread, such as Nutella
2 cups buttermilk
½ cup sugar

Place the heavy cream in a saucepan over medium heat and heat, stirring, until it begins to steam. Place the egg yolks in a bowl and stir in 2 or 3 tablespoons of the hot cream. Add another tablespoon or two of the cream and stir until the yolks are warmed. Slowly pour the yolk mixture into the saucepan and cook, stirring, until it coats the back of a wooden spoon.

Remove the saucepan from the heat and whisk in the chocolate-hazelnut spread until the mixture is smooth. Strain to remove any solids, then cool to room temperature.

In a large bowl, whisk together the buttermilk and sugar until the sugar is dissolved. Whisk in the cooled cream mixture until smooth; the cream mixture must be cool or the buttermilk may curdle. Cover and refrigerate several hours or overnight. Freeze according to your ice cream maker's instructions.

Super Simple Summer Dessert

Sometimes you need a treat on a warm day that's easy but good. Using buttermilk in this dessert balances the sweetness and gives the flavor a little something interesting.

MAKES 6 SERVINGS

2½ cups buttermilk

2 (3.4-ounce) packages instant vanilla pudding mix

4 cups whipped cream (sweetened or unsweetened, your choice)

6 cups fresh blueberries or chopped fresh peaches, or a combination

3 tablespoons granola

Mint sprigs, for garnish

Whisk together the buttermilk and pudding mix until it is smooth. Use a spatula to fold in the whipped cream. Cover and refrigerate for at least 2 hours.

To serve, alternate layers of the buttermilk mixture and fruit either in a large glass bowl or in individual glasses. When ready to serve, sprinkle the granola on top and garnish with sprigs of mint.

Janice's Gingerbread

A cup of tea and this hearty, spicy gingerbread can brighten the grayest day. And it keeps fantastically because of the moisture provided by the buttermilk. Thanks, Janice McLaughlin.

1 cup sugar
2 teaspoons cinnamon
2 teaspoons ground ginger
2 large eggs
⅓ cup melted shortening
¾ cup molasses
2½ cups buttermilk
1½ teaspoons baking soda
3 cups all-purpose flour
1 teaspoon baking powder

Preheat the oven to 325°. Spray a 9 × 13-inch baking pan with nonstick cooking spray.

In a small bowl, combine the sugar, cinnamon, ginger, eggs, and melted shortening. In a large bowl, combine the molasses, buttermilk, and baking soda. Beat until the mixture foams. Stir in the sugar mixture.

Sift the flour and baking powder together, then add it to the molasses mixture. Stir until combined. Pour the batter into the prepared pan and bake for 45 minutes, or until a toothpick inserted into the center comes out clean.

Good Things Anytime

DIPS, DRESSINGS, AND DRINKS

Use buttermilk to make beverages, dressings,
and dips into interesting additions to any meal or
party — or if you just want a good snack.

Daddy's Favorite Snack

After we had cornbread with dinner, my father liked to pad into the kitchen for a late-night treat. He'd return with a tall glass of what looked like chunky yogurt and a spoon. Then he would sit back and feast on the southern ancestor of the smoothie.

MAKES 1 SERVING

A couple of wedges of leftover cornbread
A cup or so of ice-cold, thick buttermilk

Coarsely crumble enough cornbread into a tall glass to almost fill it. Pour in enough buttermilk to moisten all the cornbread, but the mixture should still be thick and chunky. Stir a little and eat with a spoon.

Ritu's Favorite Summer Cooler

Ritu Kaur is on the staff of InterAct of Wake County in Raleigh, North Carolina, an organization I volunteer with that helps victims of domestic violence and sexual assault. Ritu is a native of India and says she craves this drink on scorching days. It's not your typical sweet smoothie but something refreshingly different.

MAKES 1 SERVING

1 cup buttermilk
¼ teaspoon ground toasted cumin seeds (see Note below)
A few pinches of salt, to taste
2–3 cubes of ice
2–3 leaves of fresh mint, chopped

Place the buttermilk, cumin, and salt in a blender with the ice. Blend until smooth. Serve with the chopped mint on top.

NOTE ❋ You can find ground toasted cumin seeds in the supermarket, but it's easy to do it yourself. Place whole seeds in a frying pan over medium heat and toss them until they are fragrant. Grind the toasted seeds in a spice grinder or in a mortar and pestle.

Mango-Spice Lassi

The South is becoming a global hot-pot of delicious flavors. Many natives of India have moved to my part of North Carolina, bringing along traditional foods. Lassi is typically made with yogurt, but buttermilk works great. If you prefer a sweeter drink, add a bit more honey.

MAKES 1 SERVING

1 cup buttermilk
1 cup frozen or fresh mango cubes
1 tablespoon honey
1/4 teaspoon cardamom
1/4 teaspoon mace

Place all the ingredients in a blender. Blend until smooth. If you prefer a thinner consistency, add a cube or two of ice.

The Vanderbilt Fugitive

This is just one of the masterpieces of the cocktail art that bar-
tender Yao Lu and co-owner Bobby Heugel create at Anvil Bar &
Refuge in Houston. The name of this drink evokes southern liter-
ary history. It refers to a group of writers who decided to challenge
and redefine the way the rest of the world viewed the South. It will
certainly make you see buttermilk differently. Use the best thick
and rich buttermilk you can find for this cocktail.

MAKES 1 SERVING

$1\frac{3}{4}$ ounces El Dorado 5 Year Old Demerara Rum
1 ounce buttermilk
$\frac{1}{2}$ ounce yellow Chartreuse
$\frac{1}{2}$ ounce Averna Amaro liqueur
$\frac{1}{2}$ ounce maple syrup
Freshly grated nutmeg, for garnish

Combine all the ingredients with ice in a cocktail shaker and
shake for at least 2–3 minutes, allowing the cocktail to expand
in volume. Strain into a collins glass containing more ice cubes.
Garnish with freshly grated nutmeg.

Avocado-Herb Dressing

Harness the power of buttermilk and make this fresh salad dressing. Adding avocado brings a special flavor and color.

MAKES ABOUT 2 CUPS

---

1 ripe avocado
1 cup buttermilk
$\frac{1}{4}$ cup sour cream
$\frac{3}{4}$ teaspoon dried savory
$\frac{3}{4}$ teaspoon dried marjoram
$\frac{1}{4}$ teaspoon salt
$\frac{1}{2}$ teaspoon black pepper
$\frac{1}{2}$ teaspoon garlic powder

Mash the avocado in a medium bowl. Add the buttermilk, sour cream, savory, marjoram, salt, pepper, and garlic powder and whisk until smooth. The dressing will keep in the refrigerator for up to 2 weeks.

Joe's Blue Cheese Dressing

Every contractor who has ever worked on my house has been a food fan. The latest, Joe Rimbey of Raleigh, North Carolina, offered his blue cheese dressing recipe, which he serves with wings. Joe uses a prepared garlic-flavored cooking creme; look for it near the cream cheese in the supermarket.

MAKES ABOUT 2 CUPS

¼ cup sour cream
½ cup buttermilk
¼ cup mayonnaise
Juice of ½ lemon (about 1 tablespoon)
1 tablespoon plus 1 teaspoon garlic-flavored cooking creme
8 ounces crumbled blue cheese, divided
Freshly ground black pepper

Place the sour cream, buttermilk, mayonnaise, lemon juice, cooking creme, and half of the blue cheese in a blender. Add a generous grinding of pepper. Purée until smooth. Remove the mixture from the blender and stir in the remaining blue cheese. Cover and refrigerate overnight for best flavor.

518 West's Buttermilk Dressing

I participate in a Scottish fiddle jam session at 518 West Italian Café in downtown Raleigh, North Carolina. Yes, you read that right—Scottish music at an Italian restaurant. No haggis on the menu though, just good, casual Mediterranean food. Chef Blaine Nierman provided this recipe.

MAKES ABOUT 2 ½ CUPS

1 cup mayonnaise

1 cup buttermilk

1⅛ teaspoons chopped garlic

¼ cup diced yellow onion

3 tablespoons Dijon mustard

1⅛ teaspoons salt

¼ teaspoon black pepper

2 tablespoons chopped parsley

In a large bowl, stir together all the ingredients. Cover and refrigerate.

Roasted Sweet Onion and Garlic Dip

I've been on a quest to make an improved onion dip, one that I can feel less ashamed about snarfing while watching basketball games than the stuff in the tub. Buttermilk makes all the difference.

MAKES ABOUT 1½ CUPS

1 sweet onion, such as Vidalia
1 head garlic
Olive oil
1 teaspoon chopped fresh dill
½ teaspoon dried thyme
¾ cup buttermilk
2 tablespoons sour cream
¾ teaspoon salt
¾ teaspoon black pepper
¼ teaspoon ground mustard

Preheat the oven to 425°. Lay out 2 doubled pieces of aluminum foil. Place the onion in one piece and the garlic in the other and drizzle both with a little olive oil. Wrap each one tightly, place them on a baking sheet, and roast for 45 minutes to 1 hour. The onion may take slightly longer to roast than the garlic. Remove each from the foil and let cool to room temperature or wrap tightly and refrigerate for up to 2 days.

Remove the outer skin from the roasted onion and place the onion in a blender. Press the roasted garlic cloves out of their skins and add them to the blender. Add the dill, thyme, buttermilk, sour cream, salt, pepper, and ground mustard. Purée until smooth. Cover and refrigerate.

NOTE ❋ If you want a thinner consistency for a salad dressing, add a little more buttermilk.

Lynn's Homemade Ricotta

I made a horrible mess the first time I tried to make my own ricotta cheese. But under Lynn Taddeo's excellent tutelage, I am now cranking it out. Buttermilk adds flavor and helps the curds form without adding vinegar. And there is nothing like the taste of the fresh stuff. Lynn, who lives in Garner, North Carolina, is the brains behind linacucina.com, her baking and catering site, and making ricotta is part of her Italian heritage.

MAKES ABOUT 4 CUPS

---

1 gallon whole milk (do not use fat-free, but 2 percent
    will work)
1 quart buttermilk (do not use fat-free)
1 teaspoon salt (optional)

Place the milk and buttermilk in a pot tall enough to allow the mixture to simmer and expand—you do not want this stuff to boil over on your stove. Stir in the salt, if using. Place the pot over medium-high heat.

Line a large colander with a double layer of dampened cheesecloth and place the colander in the sink. Leave enough cheesecloth to amply hang over the sides or secure the cheesecloth to the rim of the colander with a rubber band.

Stir the milk mixture every few minutes to prevent it from sticking to the pan. As it begins to heat and boil, curds will form. Adjust the heat, if necessary, to control sticking. The mixture is ready when it thickens, forms curds, and looks like wet oatmeal, which should be when it reaches about 210° to 215° on an instant-read thermometer.

Carefully pour the mixture into the colander. Let drain for 5–10 minutes, depending on whether you want a moist or a dry texture to the ricotta. The ricotta will keep for a couple of weeks in a covered container in the refrigerator.

Acknowledgments

Cookbook authors never really work alone. Not when people keep pressing their hopeful little faces to their doors and saying, "If you need any tasters . . . " I'm grateful to those who made the sacrifice for this book: Martha Waggoner; Cathy Hedberg; Chuck Small; Tom Attaway; the Weinel family; members of the neighborhood book club; my fellow fiddlers in the weekly Celtic jam session; the staff of Gentle Care Animal Hospital in Cary, North Carolina; the stylists at the Elan Group in Raleigh, North Carolina; the great booksellers of Quail Ridge Books in Raleigh; the staff of InterAct of Raleigh; my husband's coworkers at Scenera; and the fellows who framed my home addition and told me about their grandmothers' fried cornbread as they sampled mine.

A myriad of friends opened their recipe boxes and offered inspiration. Thanks to every one of them: Craig LeHoullier, Mary Turner, Martha Waggoner, Jan Norris, Magie Lanz, Janice McLaughlin, Ritu Kaur, Joe Rimbey, Clara Hager, and Lynn Taddeo.

Sometimes I encountered buttermilk delights that I simply couldn't improve on. In those cases, I begged the professionals who created them for the recipes. My big thanks go to Jason Smith and Billy Apperson of 18 Seaboard in Raleigh; Brian Sonoskus of Tupelo Honey Cafe in Asheville, North Carolina; Adam Close of Blossom in Charleston, South Carolina; Blaine Nierman of 518 West in Raleigh; caterer Rochelle Myers of Harpers Ferry, West Virginia; and Bobby Heugel of Anvil Bar & Refuge in Houston.

For information on the science of buttermilk and dairy products, I thank the North Carolina State University Department of Food, Bioprocessing and Nutrition Sciences, in particular Lynn G. Turner. (The treats from Howling Cow Ice Cream weren't bad, either.)

I'm grateful to my food-writing colleagues Kathleen Purvis and Andrea Weigl and fellow members of the Association of Food Journalists for not rolling their eyes during my dozens of conversations about buttermilk.

This is my fifth cookbook, and I can tell you from experience that there is nothing sweeter than a good editor. Elaine Maisner is one, and it's great to work with her and the University of North Carolina Press.

Index

a SAVOR THE SOUTH™ *cookbook*

Kathleen Purvis teaches readers how to find, store, cook, and enjoy pecans, the South's favorite nut. *Pecans* includes fifty-two recipes, ranging from traditional to inventive, from uniquely southern to distinctly international, including Bourbon-Orange Pecans, Buttermilk-Pecan Chicken, Pecan Pralines, and Leche Quemada. In addition to the recipes, Purvis delights readers with the pecan's culinary history and its intimate connections with southern culture and foodways. Headnotes for the recipes offer humorous personal stories and preparation tips.

"One of the foremost voices in southern food writing celebrates the South's iconic nut—and does it proud."
—Damon Lee Fowler, author of
Classical Southern Cooking and *The Savannah Cookbook*

We'll be serving up new SAVOR THE SOUTH™ cookbooks each season—including *Tomatoes, Peaches, Biscuits, Catfish,* and more.